1956
Railways &
Recollections

Contents

Introduction	3
British Railways narrow gauge...	5
The Severn Venturer	16
The line to Wells on Sea	18
A Gricer's idea of paradise	20
Special trains and tours	31
Out and about roaming the rails	34
Tank engines at rest and at work	41
Dawn of the diesels	46
Happenings:	
1956 Railway Happenings (1)	4
1956 Films a selection	6
1956 UK No 1 Records	11
1956 Railway Happenings (2)	15
1956 Happenings	27, 29, 39
Index & Acknowledgments	48

Series Introduction

Welcome to a brand new and innovative series!

Railway publishing has been around almost as long as the railways themselves and there have been countless books with a historical theme, telling the story of a particular line, say, and occasionally linking the subject to its social context, but never before has there been, in such an accessible way, a juxtapositioning of photographic illustration of a railway subject with the events, happenings and highlights of a wider sphere and calendar. This series will, initially, take a particular year and place the views displayed alongside a carefully selected pot-pourri of what happened in that twelve-month period. The vast majority of the images in the first few books are from the Ray Ruffell collection, held by the publisher, but material from other sources will be interspersed where felt necessary

to maintain appropriate variety. Ray was a railwayman and photographer of equal merit and the main criterion for inclusion in these books is for the images to be both interesting and aesthetically pleasing within a chosen theme.

The books are aimed at a more general market than mere railway aficionados or enthusiasts and the authors hope and trust that they will be sure in their aim and that you, the reader, will find much to enjoy, appreciate, enthuse about and even smile about! And it is hoped that some of your own memories are stirred along the way and that you may wish to share these with friends!

© John Stretton and Peter Townsend 2006
Photos: © The NOSTALGIA Collection archive unless otherwise credited.

First published in 2006
ISBN 1 85794 274 4   ISBN 978 1 85794 274 3
Silver Link Publishing Ltd
The Trundle
Ringstead Road
Great Addington
Kettering
Northants NN14 4BW

Tel/Fax: 01536 330588
email: sales@nostalgiacollection.com
Website: www.nostalgiacollection.com
British Library Cataloguing in Publication Data
A catalogue record for this book is available from the British Library.
Printed and bound in Great Britain

Frontispiece **LLANFAIR CAEREINION**. A delightful scene from those halcyon days when there were fewer cars on the roads and everything seemed so much more relaxed. A group of enthusiasts relax at Llanfair Caereinion on 30 June, before enjoying a trip to Welshpool in non-standard accommodation! Opened in 1903, the Welshpool & Llanfair Light Railway passenger services ended in 1931 and freight in 1956. Bearing its GWR-allocated number, No. 822 was finally withdrawn from BR records in 1961 but, thankfully, was preserved and now runs, as *The Earl,* on the restored WLLR. *Gerald Adams*

Below **LEICESTER** Another locomotive bearing a headboard (see cover). Engine sheds were a Mecca for rail enthusiasts, as they could 'get up close and personal' to the locomotives. This is the scene at Leicester (Central) shed on 17 July, as 'A3' 60059 *Tracery,* named after the racehorse that won the 1912 St Ledger and several other major races that year and in 1913. This class of locomotive was well suited, in both names and style, to the racetracks northwards on the Great Central Railway out of Marylebone and the LNER out of King's Cross. 60059 was withdrawn in January 1963. *Gerald Adams*

Introduction
Railways & Recollections 1956

Eleven years from the end of WWII, the United Kingdom was still struggling to pull out of the ravages of the conflict, the aftermath of rationing and general lack of money. Things were about to change, however, in many areas.

Two major crises in this year were the Suez Crisis when, on 26 July, Nasser nationalised the Canal for Egypt. The political fall-out was to claim Prime Minister Anthony Eden's scalp the following year. 1956 was also the year when the Soviet Union invaded Hungary in answer to that country's protests against Communist rule and plans to become a neutral state. Khrushchev's put down of the revolt was bloody and brutal. On a slightly happier note, Tunisia obtained independence from France in this year.

Personalities born this year were actors Mel Gibson, Tom Hanks and Bo Derek, and subsequent tennis stars Bjorn Borg and Martina Navratilova. A new phenomenon took hold and two other household names were making news this year, one on the way out and one on the way in! Bill Haley began the year five weeks into his seven-week stint at the top of the charts with Rock Around The Clock but, despite six other records in the Hit Parade during the year, none emulated this first and his star was on the wane. By contrast, Elvis Presley made his first entry to the charts in May (with Heartbreak Hotel), heralding the real arrival of 'Rock 'n' Roll', which was to sweep all before it over the next few years. He had six entries in 1956 but, incredibly in hindsight, No.2 was the highest position reached. At this time he was up against established stars Tennessee Ernie Ford, Dean Martin, The Dream Weavers, Kay Starr, Winifred Attwell and Ronnie Hilton. Elsewhere in entertainment, the FA Cup was won by Manchester City, 3-1 against Birmingham City.

On the UK's railways, the publication of the 1955 Modernisation Plan – and the introduction of dieselisation – was still being assimilated and assessed. Diesel shunters had been invading the system for a number of years and steam was still being built, but main line diesels were being built and would begin arriving in numbers in 1957. Pruning of the railway mileage continued and whilst no major routes were unduly affected, passenger services and even stretches of line were axed that in turn would aid the Beeching Plan within a decade. Those affected included Nottingham (Victoria)-Edwinstowe and Sutton-in-Ashfield; Yelverton-Princetown; Newport (IoW)-Sandown; Hexham-Riccarton Jct; and Welshpool-Llanfair Caereinion.

John Stretton
Oxfordshire

Peter Townsend
Northamptonshire

April 2006

1956
Railway Happenings

January The last Glasgow (Queen Street) to Edinburgh service via Coatbridge Sunnyside and Bathgate runs on 8th January.

February The Newport to Sandown line on the Isle of Wight closes

March The British Transport Commission adopts 25kV 50Hz ac overhead electrification as a standard for Britain's railways.

April Cathcart Circle electrification receives authorisation

June Third Class travel is ended on British Railways renamed Second Class!

November AWS (Automatic Warning System) receives Ministry of Transport approval.

Right **BANBURY** At its height, Banbury was graced with two stations, the one in Merton Street, adjacent to the GWR site, being the terminus for the very rural ex-LNWR branch from Verney Junction, via Buckingham and an ex-S&MJR leg from Towcester. Despite its relative small size, with just two, largely wooden platforms, it was initially empowered with a full range of facilities, even down to the ability to handle livestock, horseboxes

and 'carriages and motor cars by passenger train'! It also had a 5-ton crane. The branch from Towcester was an early casualty, with passenger services withdrawn on 2 July 1951. Traffic between Buckingham and Merton Street ended on 2 January 1961 (passengers) and 2 December 1963 (freight); and the final end for the station came on 6 June 1966. Here, 'Standard 4' 2-6-4T No.80084 waits for a run to Buckingham in 1956. *John Stretton collection*

Opposite **ABERYSTWYTH** The Vale of Rheidol Railway ran inland from Aberystwyth to Devil's Bridge, opening in 1902. Built in

the same year, No. 9 *Prince of Wales* survived incorporation into the Cambrian and then Great Western Railways and entered Swindon Works in 1924 for repairs. In truth, its state was such that it was scrapped and a completely new loco – officially known as a rebuild! – emerged as GWR No.1213. Following Nationalisation in 1948, No. 1213 became No. 9 and acquired its name, as seen here. Happily it is still active on the present day private railway. On August 20 1956, it prepares to leave the original terminus in Aberystwyth for the climb into the mountains.

1956
British Railways Narrow Gauge and the early days of preservation

1956
Films - A Selection

Title	Director
• Anastasia	Anatole Litvak
• Around the World in 80 Days	Michael Anderson
• Baby Doll	Elia Kazan
• Bus Stop	Joshua Logan
• Carousel	Henry King
• Forbidden Planet	Fred McLeod Wilcox
• Friendly Persuasion	William Wyler
• Giant	George Stevens
• Invasion of the Body Snatchers	Don Siegel
• The King and I	Walter Lang
• Lust for Life	Vincente Minnelli
• The Man Who Knew Too Much	Alfred Hitchcock
• Moby Dick	John Huston
• The Searchers	John Ford
• The Ten Commandments	Cecil B. DeMille
• Written on the Wind	Douglas Sirk

Above **ABERYSTWYTH** Another view of *Prince of Wales* at the Aberystwyth terminus on 20 August, this time seen with 'brother' No.7 *Owain Glyndwr*. In 1923, the GWR discovered that it had inherited three ex-VoR engines that, to put it mildly, were in dire need of extensive overhaul! Rather than take this route, the GW decided to build new locomotives to the original design but with Belpaire fireboxes, a heavier set of valve gear and more coal capacity. This increased the weight by 3 tons compared to the originals, but boiler pressure was also increased, from 150 to 165psi, producing a 20% increase in tractive effort. This would be very useful in later years, especially with the increase in traffic and attendant weight from its appeal to tourists.

Right **RHEIDOL FALLS** The railway has a steep climb, especially on the latter stages, to reach the higher terminus at Devil's Bridge. From Aberffrwd, roughly two-thirds of the way up, the gradient is testing, being a continuous 1-in-50 for the four miles to just short of the terminus. In former years the views over the valley were stunning but, sadly, in recent times tree growth has shielded these from visitors. On 20 August 1956, some of these views are still available and all eyes are on the valley, especially from these end two, open coaches. With the train seen near to the erstwhile Rheidol Falls Halt, the hillside seen in the left distance has born scars of old mine workings. Judging by the jumpers, headscarf, raincoats and turned up collar, this August day is not particularly summery!

Left **DEVIL'S BRIDGE** We have reached the eastern, higher terminus, at Devil's Bridge, on our trip of 20 August. The next down train stands on the right, doors open ready for the intending travellers, behind one of the trio of locos available, whilst the latest arrival has disgorged its passengers and now waits for a clear road for the loco (at the far end in this view) to run round. Note the spare coach plus van on the siding and the two other sidings, with the goods shed. Within a decade the goods shed had been demolished and by the turn of the 21st century, the two sidings on the extreme left had been lifted and the area given over to car parking. Overhanging vegetation on both sides now also restricts the view.

1956
Happenings (1)

JANUARY

- Plans for the redevelopment of London's Barbican unveiled
- Egyptian President Nasser vows to reconquer Palestine
- The 1956 Winter Olympic Games start in Cortina d'Ampezzo, Italy.
- Heroin ban effected in The United Kingdom

FEBRUARY

- *Heartbreak Hotel* provides Elvis Presley with his first ever entry in the US music charts
- Spies Guy Burgess and Donald Maclean surface in Moscow

TOWYN The Talyllyn Railway was the first narrow gauge railway in Wales to be preserved after closure, narrowly beating the Ffestiniog to the title! Seen at the Towyn Wharf terminus on 14 August, waiting to climb up the valley with its short train, No.4 *Edward Thomas* was built in 1921 for the Corris Railway. After the closure of that railway, the Talyllyn bought the loco in 1951 and restored it to working condition the following year. For many years until 2000 it ran as *Peter Sam*, a character from Rev. Awdry's *Thomas* series.

PORTMADOC. As mentioned on the previous page, the Ffestiniog Railway was close behind the Talyllyn in taking steps for preservation and eventual restoration. Both were fortunate that rails were still in situ for most of the route, but the FR had the harder task, in that the length of route was 13 miles and plans had been laid for building a new reservoir across the trackbed close to Blaenau Ffestiniog. All that is in the future, however, as 1863-vintage *Prince* stands in Portmadoc's Harbour station, prior to working a morning trip to Minffordd.

PORTMADOC Two more views of *Prince* from the same day as p.11.

The morning departure seen on the last page is again viewed here, as the elderly loco makes a spirited exit from Portmadoc and prepares to cross the Cob, seen immediately in front of it. This mile-long, dead straight road and rail bearing embankment was the brainchild of William Madocks, MP for Boston, Lincolnshire, who had great plans for a quicker route than previously available between London and Ireland and for this to pass through his land at what would become the townships of Portmadoc and Tremadoc (both named after him). Begun in 1806, to dam the notoriously tidal Traeth Mawr estuary, opening was to be September 1811, but was delayed when a gale and unusually high tide breached the new structure roughly mid-way. Today, railway and visitor alike take it all for granted!

PORTMADOC Turning through 180° and looking back towards Harbour station, watched closely by the young child in its coach built pram, *Prince* once again draws out of the platform, this time with an early afternoon departure.

The restorationists finally secured ownership of the moribund FR in 1954, with passenger services beginning the following year. Much redundant stock, which had literally been abandoned in the station sidings on closure in 1946, had to be cleared, together with attention to the state of the track, the Cob and the line cleared to Boston Lodge Works, at the far end of the Cob, and then up to Minffordd, the next station up the line.

All of this – and subsequent advances – were not without their own snags and problems, but the railway volunteers (and, later, some paid staff) persevered and the final goal of Blaenau Ffestiniog, 13 miles away, was reached in 1982.

It is frequently overlooked by visitors that the railway was laid out from the 1860s to be a continuous down gradient from Blaenau, enabling 'gravity trains', loaded with slate to travel to the port from the quarries. These trains are still re-enacted during Galas and special events and are fascinating to lineside spectators!

DOLGOCH Briefly returning to the Talyllyn, we have another view of No.4 *Edward Thomas*, proudly displaying a destination headboard and stopping for water en-route at Dolgoch, on 25 July. Note the fashions on display – staid by today's standards but with floral dress, shorts and two-tone jumper (right) beginning to show some colour and design as the country recovered from wartime and rationing.

Built initially by Kerr, Stuart & Co. Ltd, the name was given on restoration by Hunslet Engine Co., to celebrate a former manager. From 1958 until 1969, the loco ran with a Giesel ejector in place of its normal chimney – the first such installation in the British Isles.

Its former red livery was replaced in 2000 by BR black, followed by unlined green in 2004, following an extensive overhaul but, at the time of writing, it now wears standard TR livery of deep bronze lined with yellow lining and black borders. *Gerald Adams*

1956
Happenings (2)

FEBRUARY

- British Foreign Minister John Selwyn Lloyd embarks on Middle East peace trip visiting Egypt, Pakistan and India

MARCH

- Lieutenant General John Bagot Glubb commanding officer of the Arab Legion sacked by King Hussein of Jordan
- Archbishop Makarios deported from Cyprus by British Government
- Pakistan becomes the first Islamic republic.
- Riots erupt in Cyprus over Archbishop Makarios deportation issue

APRIL

- Spain gives up its protectorate in Morocco
- British diver Lionel 'Buster' Crabb vanishes while diving in Portsmouth harbour to investigate visiting Soviet cruiser on good will visit to the UK. A mystery that has spurned numerous theories to this day. (Cabinet Papers retained on extended secrets list until 2057)
- Grace Kelly the Hollywood actress marries Prince Rainier of Monaco (19 April)

1956
Catch it while you can!
The Severn Venturer

Below **THORNBURY** Railtours have long been popular with enthusiasts and, on occasions, even with the general public! One that proved to be very popular was the Railway Enthusiasts' Club *The Severn Venturer*, which ran from Swindon to Serridge Junction in the Forest of Dean. As well as negotiating stretches of the ex-Severn & Wye Railway, from Berkeley Road through Lydney and Parkend to Serridge Junction, it also visited the endangered branches from Yate to Thornbury and Dudbridge to Stroud (Wallbridge). Built by BR to basically a GWR

design, '1600' Class 0-6-0PT No.1625 stands at Thornbury on 15 April, before running round its train. The station had been closed to passengers in June 1944, with complete closure on 30 September 1967.

Inset above **STROUD (Wallbridge).** Another glimpse of 1625 on the REC tour on 15 April, this time at the terminus at Stroud (Wallbridge). The visitors make the most of the rare opportunity to explore the station, closed to passengers in June 1947; total closure came on 1 June 1966.

1956 Arrivals & Departures

Births

- Mel Gibson   actor and director   *January 3*
- Paul Young   musician   *January 17*
- Johnny Rotten   singer   *January 31*
- Sue Barker   TV presenter   *April 19*
- Koo Stark   actress   *April 26*
- Olga Korbut   gymnast   *May 16*
- Sugar Ray Leonard   boxer   *May 17*
- Björn Borg,   tennis player   *June 6*
- Patricia Cornwell   novelist   *June 9*
- Jerry Hall   model and actress   *July 2*
- Tom Hanks   actor   *July 9*
- Ray Wilkins   footballer and coach   *September 14*
- Amanda Burton   actress   *October 10*
- Martina Navratilova   tennis player   *October 18*
- Nigel Kennedy   violinist   *December 28*

Deaths

- Sir Alexander Korda   *film director*   (b. 1893)   24 January
- A. A. Milne   *author*   (b. 1882)   31 February
- Robert Newton   *actor*   (b. 1905)   25 March
- Alben Barkley   *US Vice President*   (b. 1877)   30 April
- Maurice Tate   *Cricketer*   (b. 1895)   18 May
- Jackson Pollock   *painter*   (b. 1912)   11 August
- Bela Lugosi   *actor*   (b. 1882)   16 August
- Peaches Browning   *actress*   (b. 1910)   23 August
- Anastasio Somoza García   *President of Nicaragua*   (b. 1896)   21 September

Left **WELLS ON SEA** was on the end of the ex-GER branches from Heacham to the west and Fakenham to the south. Passenger services from the whole of the former were withdrawn on 6 June 1952, (with freight from Wells to Burnham Market on the same day), so the brand new DMU set, featuring Motor Brake

Second 79048 nearest the camera, seen on 5 April would be part of a drive to reduce costs on the Fakenham/Dereham run. This obviously did not work, however, as both passenger and freight were withdrawn in this direction on 5 October 1964, leaving Wells devoid of rail access.

Below To the right of the platform, in the view of p.18, stands the engine/goods shed, erected in 1857 at the opening of the station. Here it is empty, as it officially closed in September 1955, but it continued to serve incoming steam locos for at least another five years – and it stood until closure of the line in 1964. The station nameboard is prominent here – although known in official circles as Wells-next-the-Sea! – with ex-GER 0-6-0 (LNER Class J17) No. 65573 in the shed yard on 5 April, simmering quietly before returning south. Coal wagons inhabit the siding, extreme left.

1956
Catch it while you can!
The line to Wells On Sea

WOLVERHAMPTON (Stafford Road)
A wonderful example of a gricer's paradise!
Seen through the railway arch on 19 August,
the shed yard at Wolverhampton Stafford Road
(code 84A) is full of activity, with both men and
machines 'raring to go'!

Nearest the camera is 'Hall' 4976 *Warfield Hall,*
a somewhat rare visitor at this time, being
allocated to Laira (Plymouth) shed! Perhaps
a visit to the Works at Stafford Road was the
reason. The rest of the yard is full of other
express locomotives, some with plenty of
steam available, with just one 94xx 0-6-0PT
indulging in a spot of shunting (centre).
Gerald Adams

1956
Happenings (3)

MAY
- R. H. Turton, Health Minister, rejects calls
  for a Government led anti-smoking
  campaign.
- First air-borne explosion of a hydrogen
  bomb at Bikini Atoll
- The first Eurovision Song Contest* held
  in Lugano, Switzerland The first winner was
  Lys Assia (Switzerland) with her song *Refrain*
  * Known initially as The Eurovision Grand Prix

JUNE
- 1956 Summer Olympics: Equestrian events
  open in Stockholm, Sweden

1956
A Gricer's idea of
Paradise?
Locomotives on shed

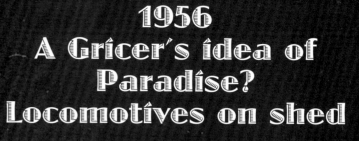

SEVERN TUNNEL JUNCTION
Larger engine sheds were sited, not surprisingly, at locations where work was such that greater numbers of locos and/or types were frequent visitors. Strategic junctions of routes was an example and Severn Tunnel Junction, seen here on 2 April, was always very busy, being at the confluence of the London-South Wales main line and the route into South Wales from Gloucester. Colloquially known as 'Heavy Goods', from the type of traffic allocated to the type, 4200 Class 2-8-0T No.4298 stands in the company of other ex-GWR types, proudly displaying the Severn Tunnel Junction (86E) shedplate, three-quarters of the way through its stay at the shed in the 1950s before being moved further west. It was withdrawn from Llanelli shed on 29 June 1963. *Gerald Adams*

DONCASTER Trainspotters – local or visiting – along the East Coast Main Line (ECML) out of King's Cross were familiar with 'Streaks'- Gresley's streamlined A4's, but this loco is not quite what it seems. Originally built in 1929 to Sir Nigel Gresley's design as a 4-cylinder compound with a water-tube boiler and carrying the No.10000, the idea was not an unmitigated success and it was rebuilt to mimic his highly successful A4s in 1937. However, its wheel arrangement was 4-6-4, as opposed to the A4s' 4-6-2 and it was one of the most powerful locos within the LNER fleet, classified as 8P/7F. It was Class W1 and numbered 60700 under the nationalised British Railways in 1948. However, although giving sterling service, it suffered from being the only one of its type, with limited spares, etc. Working from King's Cross shed until November 1953, it then transferred to Doncaster, where it is seen receiving attention – with the 'gull wing' doors giving access to the smokebox – on 17 June. Withdrawal came on 20 June 1959.
Gerald Adams

OSWESTRY An old stager at a more out of the way place. The home of the Cambrian Railways, Oswestry was graced with offices, workshops and, not surprisingly, an engine shed. Even to the closure of the latter in January 1965, elderly locomotives could be found in the area and an example is here seen on shed on 29 April, with an even more elderly 'Dukedog' beyond, 'ragged up' and ready for scrap. Built at Swindon in 1897, '2301' Class 0-6-0 No.2516 is a week into redundancy, being withdrawn on 21 April, despite the apparently healthy supply of coal piled high on the tender. Thankfully, the cutter's torch was not to claim this loco and into the 21st century it was incorporated into the award-winning STEAM Museum in Swindon. *Gerald Adams*

PWLLHELI. At the other end of the Cambrian system two modern replacements for the ageing '2301' and 'Dukedog' stock stand in the yard at Pwllheli station on 23 July. With light axle loads, they were able to traverse all areas of the ex-GWR railway system, making them ideal for more rural routes. '2251' Class 0-6-0 No. 2202, left, had been a London area and then West Midlands loco until four months before this view. Here allocated to Machynlleth, it was withdrawn from that shed in October 1960. 2244 was also a Machynlleth resident at this date, having been moved to the shed at the same time as 2202, ready for the 1956 summer season along the Cambrian coast but, in contrast to its companion, there were subsequent moves to Swindon (8 September 1962) and Worcester (12 October 1964) before withdrawal in June 1965. *Gerald Adams*

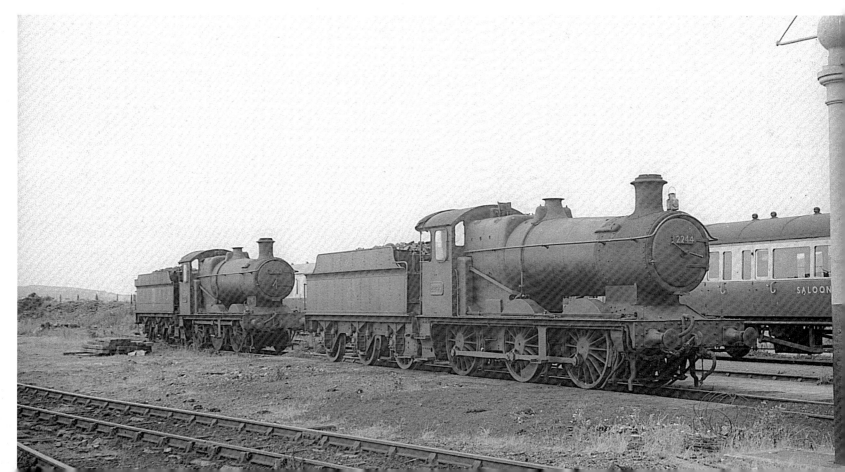

LEICESTER Another visit to Leicester (Central) shed on 15 July, again shows us A3 No.60059 *Tracery (see p.2)*. The shed clock shows 7.25; this is p.m. and the A3 waits for the road to the Central station, to take over the haulage of the northbound *The Master Cutler* express, due to depart around 8 p.m. Elsewhere in the yard are '04/8' 2-8-0 No. 63882 on the left, B1 4-6-0 No. 61128 poking out of the shed and another B1, No. 61008 *Kudu* to the right. All spent their later lives plying their trade over ex-GCR metals but whereas the first two saw the end in the Doncaster/Sheffield areas, *Kudu* experienced fresh horizons from 16 March 1963, when it was transferred to Scotland, first to Eastfield (Glasgow) and thence to Carstairs, from where the end came on the very last day of 1966. The buildings attached to the actual engine shed, of foreman's office overlooking the yard, bay window, clock and pitched roof were typical of GCR design. *Gerald Adams*

1956
Happenings (4)

JUNE

- MP Sydney Silverman's bill for abolition of the death penalty passed by the House of Commons.
- Marilyn Monroe marries the playwright Arthur Miller on June 29

JULY
- The House of Lords defeats the Bill to abolish the death penalty
- Egypt nationalises the Suez Canal sparking international condemnation.
- At Old Trafford Jim Laker breaks previous record (17) in the fourth Test by taking 19 wickets in a first class match.

Left **WOLVERHAMPTON (STAFFORD ROAD)** A second brief look at Wolverhampton (Stafford Road) shed on 19 August, shows 'King' Class 6024 *King Edward I.* New from Swindon in June 1930, it is here still with its original single chimney (a double version was fitted in March 1957). Finally running a total of 1,570,015 miles before withdrawal from Cardiff (Canton) shed in June 1962, it happily escaped the railway's Grim Reaper, to enter preservation. Based at Didcot Railway Centre at the time of writing, it can often be seen out on the main line, recreating exciting views from the past. *Gerald Adams*

WREXHAM Three distinct styles of loco stand just outside Wrexham's Rhosddu shed building on 29 April. Left to right are: 'Standard 2' 2-6-2T No. 84003, built for light/branch line passenger duties; William Stanier's LMS equivalent but type 3 2-6-2T No. 40086; and ex-LNER Class N5 0-6-2T No. 69362. The latter would appear to be an interloper but, in truth, the shed could more correctly be called LNER, being an ex-GCR facility in the midst of ex-LNWR and ex-GWR territory, standing at the end of a long branch from Birkenhead! The exposed wall to the right evidences the reduction in overall coverage effected by BR in the early 1950s; the shed closed on 4 January 1960 and was demolished not long after.
Gerald Adams

WREXHAM. Another view of the ex-GCR shed at Wrexham Rhosddu shows a second N5 on 29 April. This time, however, No.69335 is not about to return to work in a hurry, as it is lifted with the aid of the sheer legs behind, for attention to the rear end. Having worked in and around Manchester until May 1955, the loco then came to Wrexham to haul local Denbighshire passenger turns, but only lasted until 5 October 1957. *Gerald Adams*

1956
Happenings (5)

AUGUST

- West Germany bans communist party
- Television broadcasts start in Nicaragua

SEPTEMBER

- Submarine telephone cable (TAT 1) between UK and the United Staes and Canada becomes operational
- *Armchair Theatre* starts on Sunday nights on ITV network and runs until 1968 in original form

OCTOBER

- RAF retires its last Lancaster bomber from active service. (The Battle of Britain Flight's *City of Lincoln* Lancaster PA474 was loaned in 1952 to Flight Refuelling Ltd subsequently returning to the RAF)
- Suez Crisis starts as Israel invades the Sinai Peninsula. Egyptian forces are pushed back toward the Suez Canal.
- The United Kingdom and France begin bombing Egypt to force the reopening of the Suez Canal.
- Hungarian uprising against Soviet rule brings fighting to the streets of the capital Budapest and quickly spreads to other parts of the country

Left **OSWESTRY.** On p.1 we saw ex-GWR and Welshpool & Llanfair Railway loco No.822 *The Earl.* In this view, we have the sister loco, No.823 *The Countess,* safely ensconced inside Oswestry Works. With its home railway closed in this year, it is interesting to speculate whether *Countess* was brought in for repairs before closure – and was, therefore, overtaken by fate! – or whether, instead, that fate was recognised and the loco was brought in for restoration ready for preservation. Whatever the reason, No.823 actually remained on BR's books until July 1962 and, like No.822, runs on the present day WLLR!

A contrast in this little loco's fortunes, she looks somewhat forlorn in this picture, was to materialise on 19 July 2002 when No 823 had the honour of pulling the WLLR's first Royal Train. The Prince of Wales travelled on her footplate from Golfa to Welshpool.
The Countess carried the original Cambrian Railways headboard used in 1896, when the then Prince of Wales travelled to Aberystwyth.
Gerald Adams

1956 Special Trains and Tours

Below **EDINBURGH.** The date is 2 August and the brand new Metro Cammell DMU sets have been working passenger turns around Edinburgh for less than two months. Thus, the gang of workmen on the track alongside the newcomer are transfixed by this apparition as it passes Portobello Goods Yard and ex-LNER Class N15 No.69148. The bridge behind carries the Portobello-Millerhill line.
John Stretton collection

Left **DONCASTER.** Midland Compound 4P 4-4-0 No. 40928 stands in Doncaster station on 17 June, shortly after 1.10 p.m., having brought in the SLS Special from Birmingham (New Street). Members of the tour will have a little under three hours to enjoy their organised visit to Doncaster Works and will no doubt see many fascinating sights before they rejoin the train for a 4 p.m. departure for York, where a visit to the Museum and engine sheds was arranged. Return to Birmingham was due by 9.47 p.m.!

No 40928, here seen in highly serviceable condition and no doubt about to take advantage of the water column next to it, was a Birmingham engine the whole of its BR life, being withdrawn on 22 March 1958.
Gerald Adams

Opposite **HEREFORD.** Another SLS Special, this time a little later in the year. On a very dull 9 September, 'Star' 4-6-0 No. 4056 *Princess Margaret* has arrived at Hereford Barton around midday and pauses to take water, en-route from Birmingham (New Street) to Swindon Works, via Severn Tunnel Junction. Return was to be by way of Stratford-on-Avon, with arrival in Birmingham at 9.10 p.m.

The last of this elderly class to survive, 4056 was a Bristol (Bath Road) loco from prior to Nationalisation through to final withdrawal on 5 October 1957. *Gerald Adams*

SMETHWICK Through the 'Railway Mania' of the mid- to late-Victorian years, lines seemed to spring up anywhere and everywhere, often crossing those of competing Railways, as seen here. On 23 March, '5700' Class 0-6-0PT No. 8797 earns its keep by hauling a mixed freight towards Smethwick Junction station and possibly bound for the nearby Oldbury Goods terminus. Running on ex-GWR metals the rake is about to cross Galton Bridge, over the ex-LNWR Wolverhampton-Birmingham (New Street) main line. To the right, the Birmingham Canal passes under the graceful arch.
Gerald Adams

1956
Out and about roaming the rails...

Below **LEICESTER.** In the early years of the 20th century many of our railways were developing ever bigger and more powerful locomotives, with the exception of the LMS, which had a 'small engine policy'. A result of this was the proliferation of 'double heading' on express and/or longer trains. An unidentified date in early summer sees '2P' 4-4-0 40396, with another loco of the class in tow, powering away from Leicester with a local train bound for Burton-on-Trent. To the left is the little known Welford Road platform, where, in the early days of the line, trains would pause to have tickets checked before entering Leicester's London Road station just a few hundred yards further on! *J F Clay, John Stretton collection*

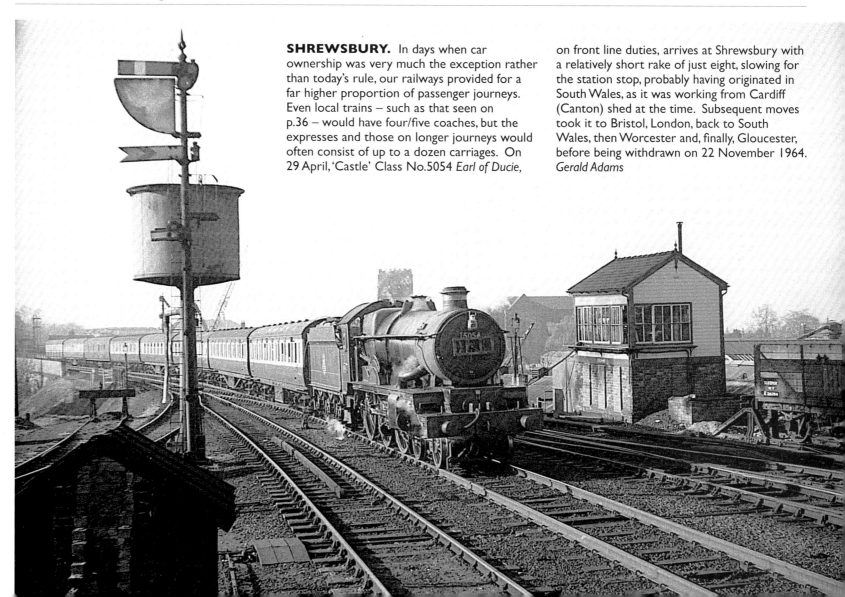

SHREWSBURY. In days when car ownership was very much the exception rather than today's rule, our railways provided for a far higher proportion of passenger journeys. Even local trains – such as that seen on p.36 – would have four/five coaches, but the expresses and those on longer journeys would often consist of up to a dozen carriages. On 29 April, 'Castle' Class No.5054 *Earl of Ducie*, on front line duties, arrives at Shrewsbury with a relatively short rake of just eight, slowing for the station stop, probably having originated in South Wales, as it was working from Cardiff (Canton) shed at the time. Subsequent moves took it to Bristol, London, back to South Wales, then Worcester and, finally, Gloucester, before being withdrawn on 22 November 1964. *Gerald Adams*

Below **KING'S HEATH.** In our 'centrally heated' era, it is often easy to overlook and/or forget some of the adverse conditions that our railways have to deal with. Men working on the track or infrastructure still have to cope with the vagaries of our weather but, in steam days, the loco crews too had their own problems. Breaking frozen coal, watering their steeds or standing on the footplate in a biting wind, for

example, was no joke and, no doubt, the crew of Fowler-designed '4F' 0-6-0 No. 43863 would be sheltering in the cab as close to the engine's fire as possible, as they pass King's Heath, south of Birmingham, on a decidedly wintry-looking 14 February. *Gerald Adams*

Opposite **SMETHWICK.** We return here to Smethwick, previously seen on p.34. Using the

same vantage point as on that page, but looking in the opposite direction, the ex-LNWR route is again seen, with the Birmingham Canal this time to the left. On 29 March, ex-LNWR '7F' 0-8-0 No. 49313 heads north, seemingly in no hurry with its short goods train and attempting to blot out the weak early spring sunshine with its exhaust! *Gerald Adams*

1956
Happenings (5)

NOVEMBER

- Soviet troops restore control in Hungary
- British and Allied forces take control of Suez
- Dwight D. Eisenhower (Republican) is re-elected as US President with record share of the vote
- UN Resolution calls for Britain, France and Israel to withdraw their troops from Arab lands with immediate effect.

- The 1956 Summer Olympic Games start in Melbourne Australia

- Petrol rationing hits Britain due to the Suez Crisis, causes panic buying to break out

DECEMBER

- *Pea-souper* Fog hits many parts of Britain causing death on roads
- The *Granma* docks in Cuba carrying Fidel Castro and his supporters
- British and French forces leave Suez Canal region
- United Kingdom end the Olympics in 8th place winning 6 Gold, 7 Silver and 11 Bronze medals

CLIFTON DOWN. Another example of the level of facilities granted to passengers in our period. The train is destined to travel only a handful of miles on the northeast suburbs of Bristol, but still there are at least four carriages, giving ample accommodation for travellers. On an unknown summer day, an equally unidentified '5700' Class 0-6-0PT member restarts a Temple Meads-Severn Beach local away from Clifton Down, with some of Bristol's substantial dwellings behind. Note, also, the extensive goods yard for this small suburban station. *John Stretton collection*

BRISTOL. Not surprisingly, gleaming express steam engines at the head of trains, often with exciting or fascinating names, were favourites with thousands of small boys but the railways were also in need of types to undertake more menial tasks. These often fell to tank locos, that could negotiate tighter curves and were well suited to hauling often lighter loads (though not exclusively) over shorter distances. The LMS 0-6-0T 'Jinties' were well loved by crews and enthusiasts alike after their introduction in 1924. No. 47552 is here seen on Bristol (Barrow Road) shed on 18 March, in company with a much earlier design. *Gerald Adams*

1956
Tank Engines at rest and at work

BLACKHEATH. For loads that were heavier or required to be moved over longer distances, heavier goods locos were designed and these also included tank versions. On 27 September, '5600' Class 0-6-2T No. 5658 trundles past Blackheath, near Birmingham, with a decidedly mixed rake of wagons and box vans. Largely designed for South Wales coal traffic, members of the class did spread their wings. *Gerald Adams*

DIDCOT. Yet another facet to their work is seen here, as an unidentified tank is hard at work moving a much larger loco around the shed yard. A highly unusual visitor to this GWR heartland, it would be interesting to learn the reason for the presence of Class S15 4-6-0 No. 30500, which is in light steam. Driver R Lethbridge is here either anxious at the position of the photographer or is keen to have his portrait recorded as the movement is undertaken. With Ray Ruffell, the photographer, being a railway employee, it could well be the latter!

PWLLHELI. A picture full of interest, fascination and unanswered questions! The scene is Pwllheli on 23 July and there is a lot going on. '4500' Class 2-6-2T No. 4549, to the left, stands on one road with just a couple of 16ton wagons, while a fellow class member has two brakevans on the adjacent road and a third member of the class sits by the water tower. There is casual examination of one of the two 16ton wagons, but much more intense consideration is being given to some point among the group by the water tower, watched by the driver of the centre loco. Captions on a postcard, please! *Gerald Adams*

Right **BRISTOL.** Dieselisation on our railways was explored prior to World War 2, with shunters being built by a number of disparate organisations from 1933, but 'mass production' didn't begin until shortly before the outbreak of war. LMS Derby Works turned out its second shunter (after a prototype five years earlier) in May 1939, continued until 1942 and then restarted in April 1945. Other railways followed the LMS lead, but squadron construction by BR of what would become a class of over 1,000 did not begin until October 1952, when No 13000 emerged from Derby. 13187 of the type is seen here at Bristol (St Philips Marsh) shed on 18 March when just four months old. Renumbered D3187 in June 1961 and 08120 in February 1974, it was withdrawn in October 1981 and cut up at Swindon ten months later. *Gerald Adams*

Opposite **SMETHWICK.** We return to Smethwick for our last look at the railways of 1956. With the Birmingham Canal again on the right, two brand new DMU sets head for Birmingham with a local service on 14 March. Note that in those days, passengers in the front compartment could 'look over the driver's shoulder' and enjoy the view ahead; this pleasure was later denied them, when the authorities took exception to the driver being thus observed! Note also, the tall semaphore signal and the long rake of coal wagons to the left. *Gerald Adams*

1956
Dawn of the diesels

Index

Acknowledgements   48
Locos
4   10, 14
7   6
9   5, 6
822   1
823   30
1625   16, 17
2202   25
2244   25
2516   24
4056   33
4298   22
4549   44
4976   21
5054   37
5658   42
6024   27
8797   34
13187   46
30500   43
40086   28
40396   36
40928   32
43863   38
47552   41
49313   39
60059   2, 26
60700   23
61008   26
63882   26
65573   19
69148   31
69335   29
69362   28
80084   4

84003   28
Prince   11-13
DMUs   18, 31, 47

Places
Aberystwyth   5, 6
Banbury (Merton Street)   4
Blackheath   42
Bristol (Barrow Road)   41
       (St Philips Marsh)   46
Clifton Down   40
Devil's Bridge   8
Didcot   43
Dolgoch   14
Doncaster   23, 32
Hereford   33
King's Heath   38
Leicester (Central)   2, 26
          (Welford Road)   36
Llanfair Caereinion   1
Oswestry   24, 30
Portmadoc   11-13
Portobello   31
Pwllheli   25, 44
Rheidol Falls   7
Severn Tunnel Junction   22
Shrewsbury   37
Smethwick   34, 39, 47
Stroud (Wallbridge)   17
Thornbury   16
Towyn   10
Wells on Sea   18, 19
Wolverhampton (Stafford Road)   20, 21, 27
Wrexham (Rhosddu)   28, 29

Acknowledgements

As with projects of any size and/or complexity, there are many people 'behind the scenes' who give of their time, expertise, advice, etc. willingly but often receive little in the way of thanks in return. The same is true with this new series, with the exception that the team putting the launch titles together has been smaller than is the norm.

There have been others 'in the wings', but the core personalities who deserve especial mention – apart from the two authors, whose patience, tolerance and friendship have somehow survived long hours, tight deadlines and frustration with some lack of information from the original photographs (!) – are Brian Morrison, for his constant and ever-ready willingness to offer assistance, advice and research facilities and for proof reading so quickly; and Sharon Rich, for her common sense approach and comments. This is her first excursion into the world of publishing and not only has it been eye-opener for her, but she has added a vital ingredient of not being an existing railway enthusiast! She has also coped remarkably well with those same tight deadlines, on top of managing her family and domestic duties!

Paul Shannon and John Vaughan deserve mention for specialist information on specific pictures.

Peter Rowlands is also thanked for his early enthusiasm, encouragement and for helping to drum up outside support; and Connie Ruffell for permission to use one or two specific photographs. Frances Townsend for sustaining her husband through the process! Without these individuals, the project would not have achieved what it already has.